Neubrandenburg

Ein Rundgang durch Straßen und Zeiten

Neubrandenburg

Ein Rundgang durch Straßen und Zeiten

Udo Zander | Jürgen Tremper

steffen verlag

NEUBRANDENBURG

Die Faszination Neubrandenburgs

„Es ist ... eins von den Bildern, die in der gegenwärtigen Zeit bald als eine Art von Märchen erscheinen werden.
... die kleine Stadt selbst, mit ihrem eichenbepflanzten Wall, ihren hohen stattlichen, in reichem gotischen Stil verzierten Toren, an deren rotem Backsteinmauerwerk hier und da wuchernde Fliederbüsche die besten Bilder gaben, ...; dann die Anspruchslosigkeit der Stadt, das stille, aber tüchtige Aussehen der Männer und Frauen und vor allem das alt bürgerliche echt deutsche Hauswesen ... Wir aber genossen Zug für Zug aus diesem romantischen Becher!“ [1]

Diese Impressionen notierte Carl Gustav Carus (1789-1869) fast ein halbes Jahrhundert nach seinem Kurzaufenthalt in Neubrandenburg. Er hatte sich 1819 mit dem Maler Caspar David Friedrich (1774-1840) mit einer gewöhnlichen Postkutsche von Berlin aus auf dem Weg zur Insel Rügen gemacht. Einige Jahre zuvor hatte die Stadt am Tollensesee bereits Caspar David Friedrich fasziniert. Um 1816/1817 hat er „Neubrandenburg im Morgennebel“, 1835 „Sonnenuntergang bei Neubrandenburg“ gemalt.

Solch empfindsame Eindrücke finden sich aus vielen Epochen.

Andere Meister ihres Faches kamen und kommen in die Stadt nahe am Tollensesee, hinterlassen ihre großen und kleinen Denkmale in Baukunst, Malerei, Literatur und Film.

Was hat die Meister der Kunst an der kleinen Landstadt fasziniert? Wahrscheinlich das bezaubernde Antlitz der Stadtmitte.

Das Antlitz

Bis in die Gegenwart imponieren die vier Tore, die Wiekhäuser, der Wall, die Backsteinbauten und andere steinerne Belege vergangener Zeitalter den Fremden wie auch den Einheimischen. Fast schon vergessene Züge einer Vorderstadt scheinen immer wieder auf. Die modernen Wanderer nähern sich heutzutage nicht mit vier oder sechs Pferdestärken, eher mit achtzig, hundert und noch mehr Pferdestärken der drittgrößten Stadt in Mecklenburg-Vorpommern. Sie alle fahren, ja schweben über eiszeitlich geprägte Hügel und Anhöhen der reizvollen Landschaft Mecklenburgische Seenplatte, bis ihnen aus drei Himmelsrichtungen Neubrandenburg in malerischer Tallage zu Füßen liegt.

Mittendrin die Perle Altstadt. In den vergangenen Jahrhunderten einige Male wieder erstanden nach zahlreichen Feuersbrünsten und Kriegsverwüstungen. Traumhaft gelegen ganz in der Nähe des Nordufers vom Tollensesee. Hier weht noch ein kräftiger Hauch von Romantik.

Wer in die Innenstadt auf den Turm der Konzertkirche oder den Turm des Hauses der Kultur und Bildung steigt, hat freien Blick auf das Besondere des mittelalterlich geprägten Zentrums. Ein Stadtrund, durchzogen von Straßen. Neubrandenburg wird von Historikern als ein „Musterbeispiel einer planmäßigen, in einem Guß entstandenen deutschrechtlichen Kolonisationsstadt angesehen. Das regelmäßige Straßengittersystem von vier nordsüdlich und fünf westöstlich verlaufenden Straßen ist aber erst im 14. Jahrhundert angelegt worden.“[2] Dass es über mehr als sechs Jahrhunderte bis heute annähernd erhalten ist, verdankt Neubrandenburg seinen Bürgermeistern, Ratsherren und Bürgern. Pittoresk wirkt die von der norddeutschen Backsteingotik geprägte Altstadt mit dem Neuen, Friedländer, Treptower und Stargarder Tor. Alle diese vier reichlich verzierten Bauwerke von europäischer Bedeutung bringen Neubrandenburg im Laufe der Zeit den Beinamen „Stadt

[1] Carl Gustav Carus. Lebenserinnerungen und Denkwürdigkeiten. Band 1. Weimar 1966. S. 207-209

[2] Volker Schmidt. Neubrandenburg. Ein historischer Führer. Hinstorff. Rostock 1997. S. 10

der vier Tore" ein. Diese Backsteinarchitektur hatte schon 1819 Carl Gustav Carus beeindruckt. „Das Material desselben ist zwar durchaus nur der gebrannte Ziegel, jedoch so gut gebrannt, daß man es wohl wagen durfte, die scharf gefügten Mauersteine frei und ohne Bewurf der Luft auszusetzen, welches dann den Gebäuden einen eigenen warmen, rotbraunen Ton gibt, der vom Witterungseinfluß allmählich in dunkelgraue Farben anmutig variiert wird. Mit diesem Material nun sind die alten Baukünstler hier in aller Weise frei und genial verfahren. Ich erwähnte schon am Treptower Tore Neubrandenburgs des hochschlanken Giebelbaues mit seinen freien Zinnen... Was aber die Kirchen selbst betrifft, so findet man die Schlankheit hoher Spitzbogen der Pfeiler und Fenster in diesem Kunstgestein oft in Wahrheit gewagter gehalten als anderswo im Naturgestein, und dabei sind die Verzierungen der Gesimse, die gegliederten Einschmiegungen der Fenster und Tore so fein und in so gutem Geschmack, daß eine eigene Sammlung gotischer Architektur aus jenen Gegenden gewiß ein erwünschtes Unternehmen sein würde, zumal da auch die Dauerhaftigkeit dieser Bauten auf eine innere Sicherheit der Konstruktion schließen läßt, aus welcher gewiß noch manches Lehrreiche für unsere Zeit zu entnehmen sein dürfte."[3]

Übrigens, das Ausgangsmaterial für die Ziegelherstellung war Lehm, damals im norddeutschen Flachland reichlich vorhanden. Es gibt im Nordosten Deutschlands keine Stadt, wo Bewohner und Touristen wie in Neubrandenburg eine mittelalterliche Stadtbefestigung im Stil der Backsteingotik erleben können. Beim Weitblick über die Stadt fällt zugleich auf, wie kräftig Neubrandenburg seit der Industrialisierung aus seinem Stadtkern heraus gewachsen ist.

Auf den Hügeln um die Stadt herum entstanden seit den 70er Jahren neue Wohngebiete und die Einwohnerzahl schnellte weiter empor. Architekten nutzten die Geländelinien der anmutigen Landschaft auf den Höhenrücken rund um das historische Stadtzentrum. Während diese Linien sanft schwingen, zeigen sich einige Bauwerke als lokale Zeugen des dramatischen 20. Jahrhunderts. Bauweisen, Stadtteilanlagen und Fassaden reflektieren Widersprüche, Spannungen, Kontraste und Brüche im Leben Neubrandenburgs.

[3] *Carl Gustav Carus. Lebenserinnerungen und Denkwürdigkeiten. Band 1. Weimar 1966. S. 211/212*

Der Lebenslauf

Wie jeder Mensch seinen ganz eigenen Lebenslauf formt, hat jede Stadt eine einzigartige Biografie. Geschrieben von vielen Generationen mit deren Arbeit, Leben und Ansichten. Ein Rundgang durch die mehr als 760jährige Stadt lässt eine eindrucksvolle Biografie erkennen und spüren. Stadtgeschichte ist fürwahr ein schwieriges Phänomen. Erst recht, wer sie in einigen Stunden oder Tagen in ihren Umrissen entdecken will.

Hier eine Historienskizze mit einigen Strichen.

Am 4. Januar 1248 verleiht der Markgraf Johann von Brandenburg zu Spandau seinem getreuen Herbord durch einen Stiftungsbrief das Recht, die Stadt zu erbauen. Mit einer vergleichsweise großen Feldmark, 200 Hufe Ackerland und 50 Hufe Weideland. Nach einer Befestigung aus Holz entsteht im 14. und 15. Jahrhundert eine steinerne Wehranlage aus Stadtmauer, Türmen, Wiekhäusern, Gräben und Wall. Diese 2.300 Meter lange Stadtbefestigung umschließt über viele Jahrhunderte bis in die Gegenwart das städtische Gemeinwesen. Handel und Handwerk treiben im Mittelalter die städtische Entwicklung zügig voran. Im Zusammenhang mit dem Niedergang der Hanse setzt im 16. Jahrhundert ein wirtschaftlicher Rückgang ein. Der Großbrand 1614, die Pestepidemie 1625 und seit 1627 der Dreißigjährige Krieg hinterlassen

Folgen im Leben mehrerer Generationen. Bränden, Unglücken und Katastrophen folgen - wie andernorts auch – immer wieder Blütezeiten. Nicht zuletzt dank der Herzogsfamilie aus dem 35 Kilometer entfernten Neustrelitz, die gegen Ende des 18. Jahrhunderts im Stadtzentrum ihren Sommerwohnsitz und das bis heute erhaltene Schauspielhaus erbauen lässt. Nach Phasen des wirtschaftlichen Niedergangs, diversen politischen Querelen und Kriegswirren ernährt sich ein großer Teil der Einwohner von der Landwirtschaft. Mit dem Anschluss Neubrandenburgs an das regionale Eisenbahnnetz zwischen 1864 und 1885 und mit fortschreitender Industrialisierung wachsen erstmalig nach 600 Jahren außerhalb der Altstadt neue Vorstädte. Bis 1918 entstehen dort mehr als 1.220 Wohnhäuser. Wie andernorts in Mecklenburg hinterlassen neu angesiedelte Rüstungsbetriebe, Kriegsgefangenenlager und Zwangsarbeit dunkle, auch blutige Spuren in der Stadtgeschichte zwischen 1933 und 1945. Am Kriegsende dominieren kahle Flächen mehr als achtzig Prozent der Innenstadt, infolge von Brand und Zerstörung. Als die Stadt der vier Tore 1952 Bezirksstadt wird, explodieren bis 1990 die Einwohnerzahlen von mehr als 25.000 auf nahezu 91.000, mit weitreichenden Konsequenzen in den Neubaugebieten. Seit 1989 sucht Neubrandenburg nach einer neuen Identität und einer stabilen Einwohnerzahl.

Die Entdeckung

Die authentische Stadtbiografie entfalten nicht nur imposante Wahrzeichen, prominente Repräsentativbauten, Straßen und Plätze, auch Wohnhäuser, Fabriken sowie Stadtteile. Sie alle versenden zugleich Flair, Atmosphäre und Esprit der Stadt. Folgen Sie uns nunmehr an Erinnerungsorte und Denkmale, in Gassen und Passagen, aber auch in Innenhöfe und Durchgänge. Wer gut zu Fuß ist, geht vielleicht auf unserer vorgeschlagenen Route. Wer mit dem Fahrrad erkunden will, entdeckt auch unaufdringliche Bilder gewöhnlicher Arbeits- und Wohnstätten. Diese Orte schildern, wie die Neubrandenburger im Alltag schaffen und leben.

Nach gut zwei, drei Stunden werden viele feststellen, keine andere Stadt gleicht der Unsrigen. Jeden Tag enthüllt sie im Wechsel der Jahreszeiten dem Einheimischen wie dem Fremden ihren Zauber. Der Gang durch Straßen wird zum Streifzug durch verschiedene Zeitalter der Stadtgeschichte.

Finden Sie selbst die einzigartigen Neubrandenburger Details im Stadtbild.

Beispielsweise in der Innenstadt die Behutsamkeit im Umgang mit dem Erbe, im Vogelviertel das Gelungene in der Sanierung der Wohnquartiere wie auch Höfe und am Bahnhof das noch zu Restaurierende.

Schauen Sie, wie die Neubrandenburger historische Umbrüche gemeistert haben.

Nun ist es aber Zeit, zu gehen und zu schauen. Durch Straßen und Zeiten. Wandern Sie und wundern Sie sich.

Dr. Jürgen Tremper

The charm of Neubrandenburg

"It is ... one of those scenes that will soon look like something out of a fairytale. ... the little town itself with its ramparts planted with oaks, its high, stately, and richly-gothic gates whose brickwork has, in places, wild lilac sprouting from it ...; then the unassuming nature of the town itself. The quiet, but competent appearance of the men and women and, most of all, the old, traditional middle-class German housing stock ...

But we enjoyed every draught from this romantic beaker." [1]

Carl Gustav Carus noted down these impressions almost half a century after his short stay in Neubrandenburg. He had set out by ordinary post coach to the island of Rugen with the painter Caspar David Fredrich in 1819. A few years before, Caspar David Friedrich had already been fascinated by the city on Lake *Tollense*. In 1816/1817 he painted *Neubrandenburg im Morgennebel* (Neubrandenburg in the Morning Mist) and in 1835 *Sonnenuntergang bei Neubrandenburg* (Sunset near Neubrandenburg). Sensitive reactions such as his can be found in many eras. Other outstanding artists came - and come - from the town near Lake *Tollense* and have left behind monuments both large and small in architecture, painting, literature and film. What was it about the little town of smallholders that fascinated them? At a guess, the enchanting aspect of the town centre.

The enchanting aspect

Right up to the present day, the four city gates, the half-timbered, square-set *Wiek*-Houses, the city wall, the brick buildings and the other stony remains of former times impress both visitors and locals. The almost forgotten features of a town built to house and protect a population that worked the fields around it keep reappearing. The present-day traveller approaches the third-biggest town in Mecklenburg-West Pomerania not with four or five horsepower, but rather with eighty, or a hundred, or more. They all drive, or rather soar, over the hills and heights of the charming landscape of the Mecklenburg lake plateau that is so marked by the ice age, until – spread picturesquely in three directions – Neubrandenburg lies below them in the valley.

In the middle is the jewel of the old town. It has been rebuilt many times over the past few centures after fires raged, or wars laid waste to it. It is just beside the northern shore of Lake *Tollense*, a beautiful spot. Here, there is still a heady scent of Romanticism.

If you climb the tower of the *Konzertkirche* or of the *Haus der Kultur und Bildung* you get a clear view of what is special about this town that was formed by the Middle Ages. It is circular and criss-crossed by streets. Historians view Neubrandenburg as a perfect example of a planned town, constructed as a piece in accordance with the regulations of the Germans who had migrated there. However, the regular grid with four streets running North-South and five West-East was only laid out in the 14th Century.[2] That it has survived more than six hundred years into the present day is due to Neubrandenburg's mayors, councillors and citizens.

The old town with its North German brick Gothic, its New Gate, Friedland, Treptow and Stargard Gates, is picturesque. All four of these richly decorated buildings, which are of European importance, have brought Neubrandenburg its nickname of 'City of Four Gates'.

The brick architecture had already impressed Carl Gustav Carus in 1819.

"The material itself is only baked brick, but so well

[1] Carl Gustav Carus. Lebenserinnerungen und Denkwürdigkeiten. Band 1. Weimar 1966. P. 207-209

[2] Volker Schmidt. Neubrandenburg. Ein historischer Führer. Hinstorff. Rostock 1997. P. 10

baked that one might dare to leave the tightly-packed stones unplastered, open to the air, which then gives the buildings a singular, red-brown tone that is delightfully varied into dark grey colours by the elements. The builders of old used this material here freely and with genius.

I have already mentioned the tall and slender building with its free-standing crenellations on the eaves of the Treptower Gate in Neubrandenburg... When it comes to the churches themselves, however, you will find that the slenderness of the high arches of the pillars and windows in this artificial stone is often more daring than that seen in buildings of natural stone, and the decoration of the cornices and the smooth, stepped insertion of the windows and doors is so fine and in such good taste that a personal collection of Gothic architecture from that part of the world would be a very desirable undertaking, especially since the longevity of the buildings points to an inner solidity of construction that would doubtless provide some useful lessons for the present day."[3]

The basic material used was clay – very easily sourced in the North German plains at that time. There is no other town in the North East of Germany where inhabitants and visitors can experience medieval city defences in the style of brick Gothic in the way that they can in Neubrandenburg. When one looks out over the town, one can also see how much Neubrandenburg has grown beyond its core since industrialisation. On the hills around the town new residential estates have been built since the 1970s and the population has grown quickly.

Architects used the natural contours of the charming landscape on the ridges around the historic town centre. While these contours have a gentle curve, some of the buildings on them bear local witness to the drama of the Twentieth Century. The facades, construction methods and sites reflect the contradictions, tensions, contracts and discontinuities in the life of Neubrandenburg.

[3] Carl Gustav Carus. Lebenserinnerungen und Denkwürdigkeiten. Band 1. Weimar 1966. P. 211/212

The biography

Just as all human beings develop their own, personal, biography, so each city has a unique story – written by many generations through their work, life and attitudes. A tour of the more than 760-year-old city allows one to recognise and feel an impressive biography. The history of a town is no easy phenomenon to grapple with, particularly if one wants to trace its outline in just a few hours or days.

This is an outline sketch of the history. On the fourth of January 1248, the Margrave Johann von Brandenburg zu Spandau gives his faithful Herbord the right to build the town. It has a relatively large area, 200 *Hufe* (one *Hufe* was between 7.5 and 20 hectares) of arable land and 50 *Hufe* of grazing land. In the 14th and 15th centuries wooden emplacements were replaced by stone defences consisting of a wall, towers, the *Wiek*-Houses, a moat and the ramparts. Over many centuries, right up until modern times, the town fortifications, 2,300 metres in length, completely enclosed the community.

Trade and crafts fired the town's development in the Middle Ages. The decline of the Hanseatic League led to economic reversal in the 16th century. The great fire in 1614, the outbreak of plague in 1625 and the Thirty Years' War, particularly from 1627, had consequences for the lives of many generations. Fires, accidents and catastrophes continue, as in many other places, to be followed by times of development and growth.

Much of the latter was thanks to the family of the Duke based in Neustrelitz, thirty-five kilometres

away. It had its summer palace built in the centre of the town at the end of the Eighteenth-Century and also built the theatre that survives to this day.
Following phases of economic decline, a number of political upsets and the chaos of wars, the majority of the inhabitants continued to earn their keep on the land. When Neubrandenburg was connected to the regional rail network between 1864 and 1885, and following increased industrialisation, new suburbs began to grow outside the old town for the first time in 600 years. By 1918, there were 1,220 homes there. Just as elsewhere in Mecklenburg, newly built arms factories, camps for prisoners of war and forced labour left dark, sometimes bloody, marks on the history of the town between 1933 and 1945.
By the end of the war, following fire and destruction, over 80 percent of the town centre had been razed. When the 'City of the Four Gates' became the local administrative centre in 1952, the number of inhabitants exploded - growing by 25,000 to nearly 91,000 in 1990, with wide-ranging consequences for the new estates. Since 1989, Neubrandenburg has been searching for a new identity and a stable number of inhabitants.

The Discovery

An authentic town biography does not only uncover imposing monuments, prestigious state buildings, streets and squares, but also homes, factories and districts. All of them give a sense of the flair, atmosphere and spirit of a town. Follow us then to monuments and memorials, down lanes and streets, but also to quiet courtyards and alleyways.
Those who are fit might want to walk our suggested route. Those who would like to explore by bike will also discover unassuming views of ordinary work and living places. These places show how the people of Neubrandenburg go about their everyday lives. After two or three hours many will find that there is no other town quite like ours. Every day, through the changing seasons, it unfolds its magic to both local and visitor alike. A walk through the streets is a trip through the various eras of the town's history.
Why not look yourself for the features of the town that make Neubrandenburg unique. For example, in the town centre, the care taken in dealing with our inheritance; in the *Vogelviertel* ('Bird Quarter'), the success in renovating the homes and the courtyards, as well as what has yet to be restored at the station. Look how the people of Neubrandenburg have managed to deal with historic upheavals. But now, it's time to go and see for yourself – through streets and through time. Wander about and wonder about it.

Dr. Jürgen Tremper

HOTEL

Unser Stadtrundgang beginnt in einer beliebten Wohngegend der Neubrandenburger. Das Jahnviertel dominieren alte Villen. Eine der imposantesten ihrer Art ist die Jugendstilvilla in der Jahnstraße 7, die nach einer umfassenden Restaurierung wieder in altem Glanz erstrahlt. Reichhaltig verziert mit Stuckmedaillons und anderen Schmuckelementen.

Our sightseeing tour starts in one of Neubrandenburgers' favoured residential areas. The Jahn-Quarter is dominated by old villas. One of the most imposing of its kind is the Art Nouveau Villa in the *Jahnstraße 7*, which after an extensive restoration glows in its renewed splendour. Richly decorated with stucco ornaments and other embellishments.

Das ehemalige Wohnhaus der Familie von Oertzen steht gleich um die Ecke. Das Familienwappen an der Straßenseite zeigt zwei geharnischte Arme, die einen Ring halten. Das Haus mit adliger Geschichte ist Teil eines Denkmal-Ensembles am Friedrich-Engels-Ring, der seit 1972 dreispurig um die Neubrandenburger Innenstadt führt.

The former dwelling of the von Oertzen family is just around the corner. The family crest facing the street shows two arms in protective armour, holding a ring. The house with aristocratic history is part of a monument ensemble at the *Friedrich-Engels-Ring*, which since 1972 has been a three-lane ring road around the inner city of Neubrandenburg.

Nebenan erinnert eine Büste aus Bronze, 1904 geschaffen von Martin Wolff (1852-1919), an „Turnvater“ Friedrich Ludwig Jahn(1778-1852). Er unterrichtete von 1803 bis 1804 als Hauslehrer die beiden ältesten Söhne des Barons le Fort. Ebenso unterwies Jahn eine Gruppe Neubrandenburger Jungen im Turnen, Wandern, Klettern und Schwimmen.

Nearby a bronze bust, made in 1904 by Martin Wolff (1852-1919), commemorates the “Father of Gymnastics” Friedrich Ludwig Jahn (1778-1852). As a tutor, he taught the two oldest sons of Baron le Fort from 1803 to 1804. Furthermore Jahn instructed a group of Neubrandenburger boys in gymnastics, hiking, climbing and swimming.

In Blickweite ist bereits das um 1400 erbaute Treptower Tor, das höchste und repräsentativste der vier Stadttore. Es kündet weithin vom Wohlstand des mittelalterlichen Neubrandenburgs und vom Stolz seiner Bürger. Das Haupttor auf der Stadtseite wurde bereits 1873 zu einem städtischen Museum ausgebaut.

Easily seen from here is the Treptow Gate, erected around 1400, the tallest and most representative of the four town gates. It announces the wealth of the Medieval Neubrandenburg and the pride of its townspeople from some distance. The main gate on the town side was already developed as a municipal museum in 1873.

Auf dem Weg in die Altstadt geht es in der 2. Ringstraße entlang der mittelalterlichen Wiekhäuser. Ursprünglich zur Verteidigung wurden bis zu 57 Wiekhäuser in die 2,3 km lange, 7,5 Meter hohe, nahezu vollständig erhaltene, mittelalterliche Stadtmauer aus Feldsteinen eingebaut. Nach dem Dreißigjährigen Krieg wurden sie zu Wohnhäusern umgestaltet.

On the way into the old town, the second *Ringstraße* passes the Medieval *Wiek*-Houses. Originally for defence purposes, up to 57 *Wiek*-Houses were built into the 2.3 km long, 7.5 metre high and almost entirely preserved city wall made from stone. After the Thirty Years' War they were converted into dwellings.

In der malerischen Ringstraße thront seit dem 15. Jahrhundert der runde, zinnenbekrönte Fangelturm. Als ihm 1845 ein Spitzhelm aufgemauert wurde, hieß er im Übrigen noch Mönchenturm. Der Oberteil des Turms beweist, dass neben Wehrhaftigkeit auch Bauästhetik eine Rolle spielte. 2005 erhielt die Haube eine Haut aus Kupferblech.

This picturesque *Ringstraße* has boasted the round, crenellated Prison Tower since the 15th century. When a conical roof was built on it in 1845, it was also called the Monks' Tower. The upper part of the tower proves that, besides the ability to resist attack, the building's aesthetic appearance played a role as well. In 2005 the peak was sheathed in copper.

Das ehemalige Franziskanerkloster ganz in Turmnähe zählt zu Neubrandenburgs ältesten und eindrucksvollen Bauten, aber auch zu den bedeutendsten Baudenkmalen in Mecklenburg-Vorpommern. Die Gründungsbauten dieses Ordenshauses gehören zu den typischen Beispielen gotischer Backsteinbauarchitektur im norddeutschen Raum.

The former Franciscan monastery close to the tower counts as one of the oldest and most impressive buildings and is one of the most important monuments in Mecklenburg-Western-Pomerania. The earliest buildings of this monastic order are typical examples of brick Gothic in the North German area.

Der Mudder - Schulten - Brunnen erinnert mit einer Szene aus dem Roman „Dörchläuchting“ – Herzog Adolf Friedrich IV. (1738-1794) von Mecklenburg-Strelitz – an den großen niederdeutschen Erzähler Fritz Reuter (1810-1874). Dieser Brunnen von Wilhelm Hans Jaeger (1888-1979) stand seit 1923 auf dem Marktplatz, ab 1961 vis-à-vis dem Fritz-Reuter-Denkmal.

The Mother Schulten Fountain commemorates the great writer of the Low German dialect Fritz Reuter (1810-1874) with a scene from the novel “Dörchläuchting” that shows Adolf Friedrich IV, Duke of Mecklenburg-Strelitz (1738-1794). This fountain by Wilhelm Hans Jaeger (1888-1979) has been situated in the market place since 1923, and since 1961 vis-à-vis the Fritz Reuter Monument.

Die Neubrandenburger spendeten 35.293,31 Mark für die Reuter-Bronzestatue, geschaffen von dem Berliner Bildhauer Martin Wolff. Der beliebte Schriftsteller hatte von 1856 bis 1863 in Neubrandenburg eine produktive wie auch glückliche Zeit in seinem Leben. „Uns Fritzing" schaut seit 1893 vom hohen Granitsockel auf Einheimische und Fremde.

The people of Neubrandenburg donated 35,293.31 Marks for the bronze statue of Reuter, created by the Berlin sculptor Martin Wolff. The popular writer had a productive as well as a happy time while living in Neubrandenburg from 1856 to 1863. "Our Fritzing" has been looking down from his high granite pedestal on both locals and visitors since 1893.

Ganz in der Nähe das Wiekhaus 8 am sogenannten „Eisenbahntor“. Es erinnert an die Zeit, als die Wiekhäuser noch als dreigeschossige Wehrtürme mit ihrer bogenförmigen Öffnung zur Stadtseite als Verteidigungsanlage dienten. Sie fungierten in Kriegszeiten sowohl als Beobachtungstürme als auch als Kampfhäuser mit etwa zehn Mann Besatzung.

A few steps from here is the *Wiek*-House 8 at the so called “Railway Gate”. It recalls the times when the *Wiek*-Houses were still three-storey fortified towers, with their arch-shaped openings towards town, functioning as defence facilities. In times of war, they were used as observation towers as well as for fighting from, and were occupied by around ten men.

Zwei Wälle und streckenweise bis zu drei Gräben gaben der mittelalterlichen Stadt zusätzlich wirkungsvollen Schutz. Dieser grüne Naturgürtel bietet als Stadtpromenade zu jeder Jahreszeit eindrückliche Naturerlebnisse wie auch überraschende Motive. Gegenüber gemahnt eine im Herbst 2008 neu gestaltete Anlage an das Schicksal der jüdischen Mitbürger; an der Stelle, wo die 1877 errichtete Synagoge in der Nacht vom 9. zum 10. November 1938 zerstört wurde.

Two ramparts and, in places, up to three moats lent the Medieval town additional effective protection. This natural green belt offers a year round opportunity to experience nature while walking round the town, as well as some surprising motifs. Opposite is a monument, newly installed in Autumn 2008, reminding one of the fate of Jewish citizens. It stands where the synagogue, which was built in 1877, was destroyed on the night of November 9-10, 1938.

Das Friedländer Tor ist die älteste, in seiner Komplexität am besten erhaltene und mit 88 Metern Länge zugleich die umfangreichste Befestigungsanlage. Das stadtseitige, 20 Meter hohe Haupttor wurde um 1300 erbaut, das Vortor nach aktuellen dendrologischen Untersuchungen 1328. Beide sind durch Mauern, einen sogenannten Zwinger, verbunden.

The Friedland Gate is the oldest, in its complexity the best preserved and, at a length of 88 metres, also the most extensive fortification. The main gate, on the town side and 20 metres in height, was erected around 1300; the outer gate was built in 1328 according to dendrological tests. They are connected by an inner bailey.

Von solcher Vollständigkeit und Zierde gibt es nur wenige Torkomplexe im nördlichen Mitteleuropa. Der dreigeschossige, acht Meter hohe Zingel war in der Vergangenheit immer wieder blutiger Kampfplatz. Die halbrunde Bastion mit ihren Schießscharten schützte das Friedländer Tor vor großkalibrigen Feuerwaffen wie ein Kugelfang.

There are only a few gate complexes in Northern Central Europe that are so complete and so ornate. The three-storey, eight metre high outer bailey was throughout history a bloody battle ground time and again. Like a backstop, the semicircular bastion with its embrasures protected the Friedland Gate against heavy-calibre firearms.

Reizvoll ist der Blick von verschiedenen Neubrandenburger Aussichtsplattformen – hier vom Ringhotel – auf die Altstadt. Im Vordergrund das Neue Tor, das jüngste der vier stattlichen Tore. Im Juli 1809 zeichnete Caspar David Friedrich (1774-1840), der große Maler der deutschen Romantik, die Stadtseite des Tores mit ihren rätselhaften Adoranten aus Terrakotta.

The view from different Neubrandenburg viewing platforms – here from the *Ringhotel* – over the old town is charming. In the foreground is the New Gate, the youngest of the four grand gates. In July 1809 Caspar David Friedrich (1774-1840), the great painter of the German Romantics, drew the town-side of the gate with its mysterious terracotta worshippers.

Wie anderswo glauben auch Neubrandenburger an einen Hauch des Zauberns der sechs volkstümlichen Glücksbringer in Schwarz. Hier auf einem Dach in der Innenstadt. Heute wie früher kehren und überprüfen sie Feuerungsanlagen. Ihre Arbeit hatte im Mittelalter eine andere Dimension, Brände in heute unvorstellbaren Ausmaßen zu verhindern.

As elsewhere, Neubrandenburgers believe in a hint of magic from the six 'good luck charms' in black. Here they are seen on a roof in the city center. Today, as in former times, they sweep and check fireplaces. In Medieval times their work had another dimension, to prevent the sorts of blazes that are unimaginable these days.

Der Rundgang führt vom jüngsten Stadttor, Sitz der Fritz-Reuter-Gesellschaft, durch die geschichtsträchtige Neutorstraße. Harmonisch fügt sich hier Altes und Neues. Reizvolle Kontraste in der Architektur faszinieren ebenso wie Lebensspuren des Maschinenbauers Ernst Heinrich Alban (1791-1856) und des Architekten Heinrich Tessenow (1876-1950).

The round tour leads from the youngest town gate, home of the Fritz Reuter Society, through the history-charged *Neutorstraße*. Here, old and new fit harmoniously together. Appealing contrasts of architecture fascinate just as much as the traces of the machinery manufacturer Ernst Heinrich Alban (1791-1856) and of the architect Heinrich Tessenow (1876-1950).

Fünf Wohn- und Geschäftshäuser in der Neutorstraße stehen auf der städtischen Denkmalliste. So auch das mit der Nummer 16. Das weithin ausstrahlende Gebäude war in seiner Geschichte auch Sitz einer Filiale der ehemaligen Reichsbank. In dieser Straße lohnt sich hier und da ein Blick in alte sowie neue Höfe.

Five residential and business buildings on *Neutorstraße* are on the municipal monument list, as is Number 16. This gleaming building was once a branch of the former *Reichsbank*. In this street the old and new courtyards here and there are worth a look.

Rathaus
Treptower Tor
Polizei

NB KR 999

An der Stargarder Straße glänzt Neubrandenburgs kostbarstes Juwel, die 1298 geweihte Marienkirche mit ihrem prunkvollen Ostgiebel. Diese vorgeblendete Maßwerkarchitektur zählt zu den kunstvollsten Schöpfungen der Backsteingotik in Norddeutschland. St. Marien erlitt durch Brände und Kriege immer wieder Schaden.

On Stargarder Street shines Neubrandenburg's most precious architectural jewel, the 1298-consecrated St. Mary's church with its magnificent east gable. This superimposed architecture of precision counts as one of the most artful creations of brick Gothic in North Germany. St. Mary's church has over time often been damaged by fire and war.

Nach Plänen des finnischen Architekten Pekka Salminen wurde in die altehrwürdige Backsteinhülle ein hochmoderner Konzertsaal eingebaut. In dieser wunderbaren Symbiose von Altem und Neuem begeistern seit dem 13. Juli 2001 international und national renommierte Orchester und Solisten das Publikum. Dank einer vorzüglichen Akustik.

An ultra-modern concert hall designed by the Finish architect Pekka Salminen has been built within the venerable brick shell. Thanks to excellent acoustics, orchestras of international and national repute, and soloists, have been thrilling audiences in this wonderful symbiosis of old and new since July 13, 2001.

Franz Christian Boll,
geboren hieselbst
am 31n August 1775,
seit dem 28n März 1802
treuer Prediger und Seelsorger
der hiesigen Marien- und
Johannis-Gemeinde,
starb
am 12n Februar 1818,

Der Obelisk für Pastor Franz Christian Boll (1775-1818), entworfen vom Caspar David Friedrich, liegt am Wege vom Marienkirchplatz zum Schauspielhaus. Das älteste erhaltene Theatergebäude Mecklenburgs hatte der Landesherr von Mecklenburg-Strelitz, Herzog Adolf Friedrich IV., um 1793 in der Pfaffenstraße erbauen lassen.

The obelisk for pastor Franz Christian Boll (1775-1818), designed by Caspar David Friedrich, lies on the way from the *Marienkirchplatz* to the *Schauspielhaus*. The oldest preserved theatre building in Mecklenburg was built on the orders of the regent of Mecklenburg-Strelitz, Duke Adolf Friedrich IV around 1793 in *Pfaffenstraße*.

In der Pfaffenstraße wird überliefertes Stadtmilieu nicht nur sichtbar, sondern auch fühlbar, erinnert an die beschauliche Vorderstadt. Bis Ende April 1945 dominierten solche kleinteiligen zwei- und dreigeschossigen Häuser das Neubrandenburger Stadtbild.

In *Pfaffenstraße*, the town's traditional background is not just visible, but palpable as well, reminding one of its history as a tranquil residential and farming town. Up to the end of April 1945 such detailed two and three-storey houses dominated the street scene of Neubrandenburg.

An der Ecke steht das Haus Stargarder Straße 35, vor etwa 200 Jahren erbaut. Hier wohnte und arbeitete Fritz Reuter von 1856 bis 1861. Von 1979 bis 1990 hatte eine Fritz-Reuter-Gedenkstätte ebenda Hüsung. Seit den 1960er Jahren betreibt Familie Fuhrmann das „*Café im Reuterhaus*“.

On the corner is *Stargarder Straße* 35, built around 200 years ago. Fritz Reuter lived and worked here from 1856 to 1861. A Fritz Reuter Memorial was housed in the building from 1979 to 1990. Since the 1960s the Fuhrmann family has run the *“Café im Reuterhaus”*.

Die nächste Sehenswürdigkeit liegt im historischen Quartier des ehemaligen Mecklenburger Fürstenhofes. Dieser attraktive Eingang in der Stargarder Straße 37 lädt in den „Fürstenkeller“ mit prächtigen Gewölben aus dem 17. und 18. Jahrhundert ein. Seit 14. Februar 1923 hat das älteste Lokal Neubrandenburgs öfters Besitzer und auch Namen gewechselt.

The next landmark is situated in the historical quarter of the former court of Mecklenburg. This attractive entrance at *Stargarder Straße 37* invites visitors to the *“Fürstenkeller”* with magnificent vaults from the 17th and 18th centuries. Operating since February 14 1923, the oldest public house in Neubrandenburg has changed owners and names several times.

In Sichtweite sind bereits neun Terrakotta Figuren in den Blendnischen des Giebels der Stargarder Toranlage zu sehen. Sie stehen seit Jahrhunderten mit erhobenen Händen in Reih' und Glied. Und keiner weiß bis heute, warum. Bei näherer Betrachtung machen sie eher einen männlichen Eindruck. Viel Raum für weitläufige Fantasien.

Within sight are nine terracotta statures in the alcoves of the gable in the Stargard Gate complex. For centuries they have stood in rank and file with arms raised, but nowadays nobody knows why. On closer examination they seem more male than female. Plenty of room for the imagination.

Frühe Stilformen norddeutscher Backsteingotik prägen die imposante Außenseite des Stargarder Vortores am südlichen Zugang zur Stadt. Das Vortor wurde in der ersten Hälfte des 14. Jahrhunderts errichtet. Es zählt zu den prächtigsten mittelalterlichen Toren in Nord- und Mitteleuropa. Wimperge und Rosetten gleichen denen am Giebel der Marienkirche.

Early styles in North German brick Gothic shape the imposing exterior of the Stargard outer gate at the southern entrance to the town. The outer gate was erected in the first half of the 14th century. It counts as one of the most magnificent Medieval gates in Northern and Central Europe. Gabled pediments and rosettes resemble those on the gable of St. Mary‘s church.

Auf dem Weg zurück in den historischen Stadtkern lohnt es, die Details zwischen den beiden Toren und den langen Zwingermauern der Anlage intensiv zu genießen. Nicht nur beim Blick durch einen kleinen Mauerbogen auf ein Wiekhaus verspürt der Stadtbesucher mittelalterliche Romantik.

On the way back into the historical city centre it is worth enjoying the details between the two gates and the long walls of the outer bailey. The visitor can sense the medieval romanticism, and not just while looking through a little wall arch at a *Wiek*-House.

Immer wieder fesseln die historischen Fassaden der sanierten und rekonstruierten Wohnhäuser in der Großen Wollweberstraße, Teil eines stimmungsvollen Ensembles. 14 Häuser stehen auf der städtischen Denkmalliste. Wie das zweigeschossige „Blaue Haus" mit Portal und Haustür. Nummer 25 wirkt als Magnet für Touristen und Fotografen.

Gegenüber bietet die Kunstsammlung in einem winkelförmigen Funktionsbau eine gelungene Synthese von spätbarockem Fachwerkbau und moderner Architektur. Der erste Museumsneubau seit 1989 in Mecklenburg-Vorpommern wurde Mitte April 2003 eröffnet. Viele Kunstschätze der ersten bürgerlichen Sammlung im Land sind seit Kriegsende verschollen.

Opposite, the art collection in its angled, purpose-built home, offers a happy mix of late Baroque timber frame work and modern architecture. The building of the first new museum since 1989 in Mecklenburg-Western Pomerania was opened in April 2003. Many art treasures of the first civic collection of the region have been missing since the end of the war.

Time and again the historical facades of the renovated and reconstructed dwellings in the *Große Wollweberstraße*, part of an atmospheric ensemble, are captivating. Fourteen of the houses are on the municipal monument list. As the two-storey *"Blue House"* with portal and front door, Number 25, is a magnet for tourists and photographs.

Ganz in der Nähe der Innenstadt steht seit 1996 das Jahnsportforum, der modernste Sporthallenkomplex im Nordosten Deutschlands. In dieser Halle trainieren Leichtathleten des Sportclubs Neubrandenburg wie Franka Dietzsch, Ralf Bartels und Petra Lammert, aber auch der Nachwuchs. Gegenüber lernen junge Athleten im neu erbauten Sportgymnasium.

Close to the inner town stands the *Jahnsportforum*, which since 1996 has been the most modern sports hall complex in northeast Germany. Athletes from the Neubrandenburg sports club such as Franka Dietzsch, Ralf Bartels and Petra Lammert train in this hall, though it is also used by up and coming sports people. Across the way, young athletes learn at the newly erected sports grammar school.

Ulrich Müther (1934-2007) und Karl Kraus entwarfen den Hyparschalenbau der Stadthalle im Kulturpark. Das Bauwerk umfasst mehr als 1.700 Quadratmeter stützenfrei überspannte Fläche. Die geschwungenen Hyparschalen zaubern seit mehr als vierzig Jahren eine elegante und zugleich imposante Mehrzweckhalle. Von Sportwettkämpfen über Kulturveranstaltungen bis zu Messen.

Ulrich Müther (1934-2007) and Karl Kraus conceptualised the *Hyparschale* building of the town hall in the *Kulturpark*. The structure includes more than 1,700 square meters of column-free spanned ceiling. The curved *Hyparschalen* have conjured up an elegant, and at the same time imposing, multipurpose hall for more than 40 years, used for sports competitions, cultural events and fairs.

Auf dem Weg durch den Kulturpark lohnt eine Kaffeepause mit Blick auf den Tollensesee, Neubrandenburgs große Badewanne. Im Lokal „Badehaus" erholen sich schon seit 1845 Einheimische und Fremde. Norbert und Liane Hein haben es als Hotel mit Restaurant und Biergarten im März 2000 wieder eröffnet.

On the way through the park it is worth taking a coffee break with a view of Lake *Tollense*, Neubrandenburg's huge 'bathtub'. Locals and foreigners have been relaxing at the public house *"Badehaus"* since 1845. Norbert und Liane Hein reopened it as a hotel with restaurant and beer garden in March 2000.

Der Tollensesee mit zwei Strandbädern, Yachthafen und Wassersportzentrum ist ein beliebtes Segelrevier. Der See bietet auf über neun Kilometer Länge und bis zu drei Kilometer Breite schöne lange Wellen, die sich beim Segeln gut ausreiten lassen.

Lake *Tollense* with two lidos, a marina and a water sports centre is a popular sailing area. The lake, over nine kilometres long and up to three kilometres wide, offers beautiful long waves to ride out on while sailing.

Ein gut ausgeschilderter Uferweg führt zum beliebten Ausflugsziel Belvedere. In Nachfolge des ehemaligen Sommerhauses der Neustrelitzer Herzöge wurde 1823/24 ein massives Gebäude in griechischer Tempelform nach einem Entwurf von Friedrich Wilhelm Buttel (1796-1869) errichtet und 1934 nach Ideen von Heinrich Tessenow in ein Ehrenmal umgestaltet.

A well signposted path along the waterside leads to the popular excursion destination Belvedere. Following on from the former summer residence of the Dukes from Neustrelitz a solid building was erected in a Greek temple style to a design by Friedrich Wilhelm Buttel (1796-1869) and reshaped as a monument in 1934 according to the ideas of Heinrich Tessenow.

Wanderer, Besucher der Veranstaltungsreihe „Sommernacht auf Belvedere“ und Gäste von Trauungen haben von der Naturterrasse einen traumhaften Blick auf den Tollensesee. Fotografen können aus dieser exponierten Lage Sport- und Freizeitsegler, Fischer bei ihrer Arbeit und Kanurennsportler beim Training mit langen Brennweiten aufnehmen.

Ramblers, visitors to the ”Summer night at Belvedere” series of events and wedding guests at ceremonies held here have a dreamlike view of Lake *Tollense* from the natural terrace. From this elevated spot, photographers with long focal length lenses can capture sport and leisure sailors, fishermen and canoeists in training.

Auf dem Rückweg in die Stadt fällt am Nordufer des Tollensesees das sanierte Amtshaus Broda auf. Es steht auf den Fundamenten und Sockeln des 1170 gestifteten und kaum vor 1240 erbauten Prämonstratenserstifts Broda, die älteste Bausubstanz der Stadt. Das damalige geistliche Zentrum der Region verfiel nach der Reformation.

On the way back into town, the renovated Broda office building on the north shore of Lake *Tollense* catches the eye. It stands on the foundation and pedestals of a monastery, founded by monks from Prémonté Broda in 1170 and built shortly before 1240, making it the oldest building in the town. The former religious centre of the region fell into ruins after the Reformation.

Von dem Ordenshaus auf dem Klosterberg sind nur noch die spätmittelalterlichen, kreuzrippengewölbten Keller erhalten, die unter dem Amtshaus liegen. Solcher Art Decken waren in der späten Gotik ein gängiger Gewölbetyp. Dessen Formen standen häufig in engem Zusammenhang mit den Mönchsorden.

Only the late Medieval, cross-rib vaulted cellars remain from the preceptory on the cloister hill, situated under the office building. Ceilings of this kind were a common type of vaulting in the late Gothic period. The shapes used were often closely related to the monastic orders.

Am Wege liegt das in den 1990er Jahren bebaute Wohngebiet Broda. Die Bewohner leben mit viel Grün und in faszinierender Nähe zum Tollensesee wie auch zu einem Waldstreifen. Sie schätzen die gute Verkehrsanbindung, die kurze Entfernung zur Hochschule, zum Kulturpark und zur Stadt sowie eine behagliche Wohnatmosphäre.

On the way lies the residential area of *Broda*, built in the 1990s. Residents live with plenty of greenery and spell-bindingly close to Lake *Tollense* and to a stretch of woodland. They appreciate the good transport connections, the short distance to the University, the *Kulturpark* and into town, and also the pleasant living atmosphere.

An Sommertagen lockt das Strandbad Broda vor allem viele junge Leute und Familien mit seinem Sandstrand sowie klarem Wasser. Im Menschengetümmel fallen Badende, Schwimmer und Freizeit-Volleyballer auf. Nicht zu vergessen, am Brodaer Strand feiern alljährlich die Neubrandenburger Schüler den letzten Schultag.

On summer days the *Broda* lido with its sandy beach and clear water particularly attracts many young people and families. Bathers, swimmers and volleyball players are in evidence among the crowds. It shouldn't be forgotten that every year the school children of Neubrandenburg celebrate their last day of school at *Broda* beach.

Vom See erreicht man in fünf Minuten zu Fuß die Hochschule Neubrandenburg, die am 1. September 1991 im Gebäude der ehemaligen Pädagogischen Hochschule gegründet wurde. Sie zählt zu den aufstrebenden Bildungsstätten des Landes. Ihr Vorteil ist ein Campus, auf dem alles nah beieinander liegt. 2009 sind hier etwa 2.400 Studenten aus dem In- und Ausland immatrikuliert.

The University of Neubrandenburg is five minutes away from the lake on foot. It was founded on September 1 1991 in the building of the former college of education and is among the up-and-coming educational institutions in the state. Being campus-based means everything is at close quarters. In 2009, about 2,400 students from home and abroad were matriculated here.

Nahezu gegenüber lockt ein kleiner, frühgotischer Backsteinbau. Die Hospitalkapelle St. Georg und ihre Nebengebäude entstanden am Beginn des 14. Jahrhunderts, um Menschen mit ansteckenden Krankheiten aufzunehmen. Das abgewalmte Dach krönt ein quadratischer Dachreiter in Fachwerk mit einer Rokoko-Laterne als Turmspitze.

Almost opposite there is a small, early Gothic brick building that catches the eye. The Hospital Chapel of St. George and its outbuildings were constructed at the beginning of the 14th century to house people with contagious diseases. The hip roof is crowned with a timber-framed square ridge turret with a rococo lantern for a spire.

Etwa 500 Meter weiter lohnt ein Blick aus der Treptower Toranlage auf die Vierrademühle. Die älteste erhaltene Stadtmühle hat eine wechselvolle Geschichte mit wechselnden Besitzern. Der sanierte Gebäudekomplex in einem Fachwerk- und Backsteinensemble erfreut sich einer großen Beliebtheit. Nicht zuletzt ob seiner Gastronomie und Feste.

Approximately 500 metres further on, the view from the Treptow Gate complex towards the *Vierrademühle* is worthwhile. The oldest preserved town mill has a colourful history with changing owners. The renovated building complex in a half-timbered and brick stone ensemble is very popular, not least because of its cuisine and feasts.

Die Inschrift verweist auf den Sohn des Stadtgründers Herbord. Bis 1998 wurde hier noch Roggen und Weizen gemahlen. Seit Frühjahr 2004 zeigt das Regionalmuseum im Obergeschoss die Dauerausstellung „Neubrandenburger Stadtgeschichte(n)" und Sonderausstellungen zu wechselnden Themen.

The inscription refers to the son of the town's founder Herbord. Until 1998 rye and wheat was still milled here. Since the spring of 2004 the local museum on the upper floor has housed the permanent exhibition – "Neubrandenburg's town (hi)stories" – and special exhibitions on various themes.

Für einen Blick in das nachgebildete Arbeitszimmer von Brigitte Reimann (1933-1973) in der Gartenstraße 6 lohnt ein Fußweg, etwa eine Viertelstunde. Die krebskranke Schriftstellerin zog 1968 aus dem in ihren Augen tristen Hoyerswerda nach Neubrandenburg in die Erdgeschosswohnung einer kleinen Villa mit Erker, Terrasse und romantischem Garten. An dieser Stelle eröffnete 1999 das neue Literaturhaus.

Seeing the reconstructed study of Brigitte Reimann (1933-1973) in the *Gartenstraße 6* is well worth the 15 minute detour. In 1968, when suffering from cancer, the writer moved from what she viewed as rather grim Hoyerswerda to Neubrandenburg into the ground floor flat of a small villa with gazebo, terrace and romantic garden. In 1999 the new house of literature opened here.

Unweit des Literaturhauses stehen die Nachbildungen des nach dem Stadtbrand 1737 erbauten Rathauses und des 1775 errichteten Großen Palais' im „Modellpark Mecklenburgische Seenplatte" am Weidenweg. In der Parkanlage verzaubern sie bis heute im Maßstab 1:25. Beide Gebäude zierten einst den Neubrandenburger Marktplatz.

Not far from the house of literature, in the "Mecklenburg Lake District Model Park" at the *Weidenweg*, are the replicas of the town hall, erected in 1737 after a town fire, and of the Great Palace that was built in 1775. In the park they continue to charm on a scale of 1:25. Both buildings once adorned Neubrandenburg's market place.

Durch ein malerisches Tal führt der Rundgang nach Neubrandenburg-Ost, das größte Stadtgebiet. Reichlich Grün, eine gute Wohnqualität in sanierten WBS 70-Wohnhäusern, die Nähe zur Natur und eine spürbar verbesserte Infrastruktur erklären die überdurchschnittlich hohe Wohndauer in diesem 1970 gegründeten Stadtteil.

Through a picturesque valley the round tour leads to *Neubrandenburg East*, the largest municipal area. Plenty of green space, a good standard of living in the renovated *WBS 70*-residential houses, the closeness of nature and a noticeable improved infrastructure explain the higher-than-average length of occupancy in this district, which was founded in 1970.

Auf dem Weg in die Nordstadt geht es an einem um 1845 errichteten Speicher vorbei. Bei dessen Sanierung wurden insgesamt mehr als 25.000 Ziegel ausgetauscht. Der von Webasto genutzte Backsteinbau präsentiert innen eine glückliche Liaison von historischen Balkenkonstruktionen und modernen Gestaltungselementen aus Glas und Stahl.

A storehouse, erected around 1845, lies on the way into the *Nordstadt*. Altogether, more than 25,000 bricks were replaced during renovation. Inside, the brick building, used by Webasto, presents a happy mix of historical timber-frame construction and modern design elements of glass and steel.

Im Quartier östlich der Ihlenfelder Straße tragen seit Mitte der 1930er Jahre zahlreiche Wohnhäuser Hauszeichen. Die 41 Zentimeter hohen und 30 Zentimeter breiten Zeichen über den Eingangstüren wurden in der Neubrandenburger Baustoff-Großhandlung Wilhelm Jaeger hergestellt. Ihre Motive lehnen sich an die germanische Runenkunst an.

In the quarter to the east of the *Ihlenfelder Straße* many of the dwellings carry emblems dating from the middle of the 1930s. The 41 cm high and 30 cm wide figures above the front doors were produced at the Neubrandenburg building material wholesale trade Wilhelm Jaeger. Their motifs refer to the Germanic art of runes.

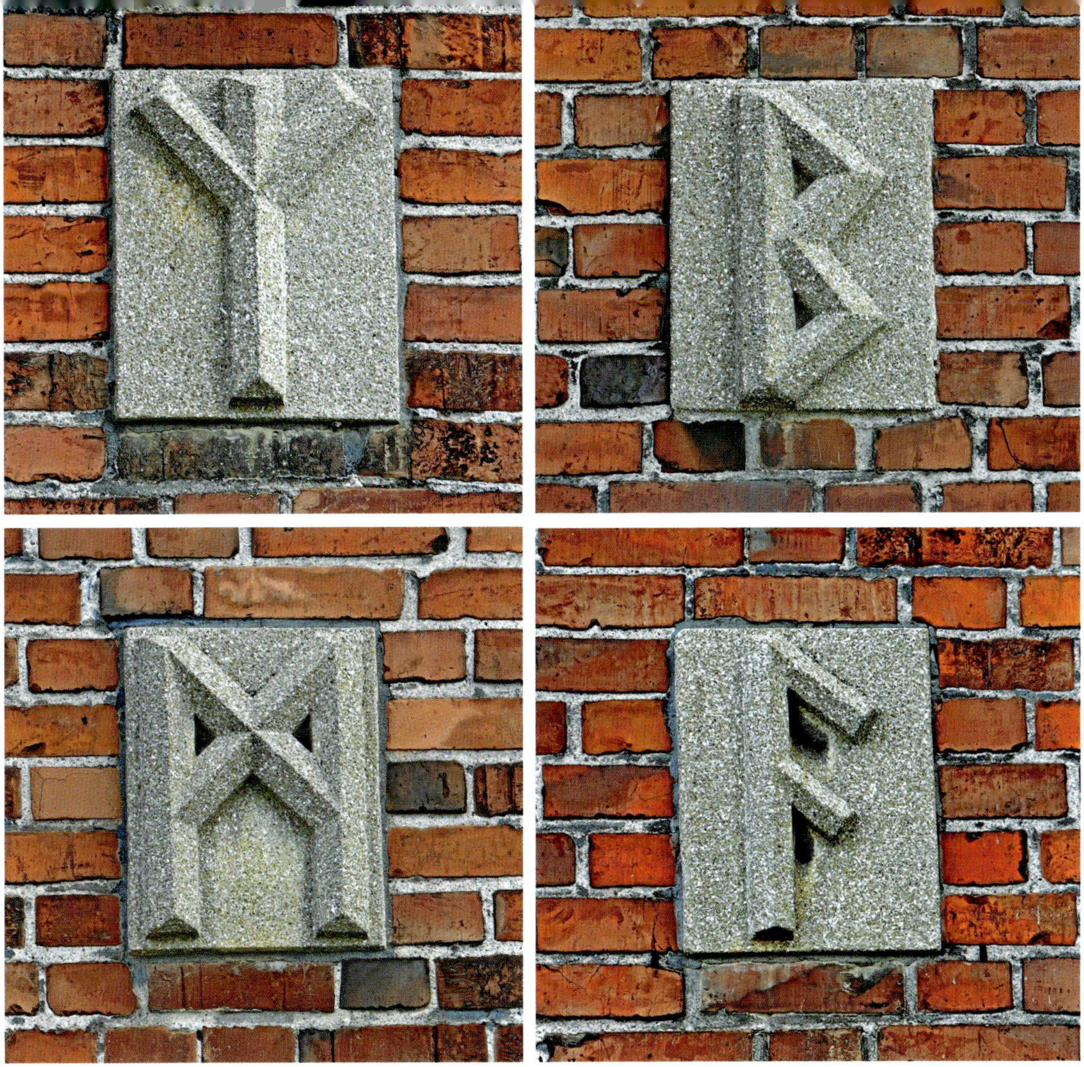

Diese vier Hausmarken in der Ihlenfelder Straße repräsentieren - jeweils von oben nach unten – die Symbole für Elch (Haus Nr. 52), Mensch (Nr. 64), Birkenreis (Nr. 50) und Ase, ein Göttergeschlecht in der nordischen Mythologie (Nr. 56). Grundlage der Deutung ist die germanische Runenreihe des älteren Futharks.

These four house emblems on *Ihlenfelder Straße* represent – starting at the top in each case – the symbol of an elk (No. 52), a human (No. 64), a birch twig (No. 50) and Ase, a deity in Nordic mythology (No. 56). The basis of the interpretation is the Germanic runic alphabet of the elder Futhark.

In der Nordstadt weisen Text- und Bild-Stelen auf vier Stationen eines Lehrpfades zur Geschichte der Zwangsarbeit vor Ort von 1939 bis 1945 hin. So das Mitte der 1930er Jahre errichtete Klinkergebäude der Mechanischen Werkstätten mit Giebel zur Demminer Straße. Nebenan war das Lager West für Kriegsgefangene.

In the *Nordstadt*, information signs with inscriptions and pictures refer to four stops on an educational trail about the history of the forced labour in the area 1939-1945. For example, the brick building of the mechanics workshops with its gable onto *Demminer Straße*, was erected in the mid 1930s. Next door was the prisoner of war camp *Lager West*.

Ein Luftbild der Ihlenfelder Vorstadt beweist, was für ein ausgedehntes Industriegelände sich im Nordosten Neubrandenburgs bis an die Innenstadt grenzend erstreckt. Zu ihm gehören die sie umgebenden Gewerbe- und Industriegebiete Warliner Straße, Industriegelände und Monckeshof.

An aerial photograph of the suburb *Ihlenfelder Vorstadt* highlights how widespread the industrial area spans from northeast Neubrandenburg to the inner city. Included in it are the surrounding commercial and industrial areas *Warliner Straße, Industriegelände* and *Monckeshof.*

Etwa eine Viertelstunde von der Demminer Straße grüßt eine Kranich-Skulptur vor dem Café „Elster“ als Wahrzeichen des beliebten Wohngebiets Vogelviertel. Die Straßen tragen, bis auf wenige Ausnahmen, die Namen von Vogelarten. Reihenhäuser, oft aus Backstein, aber auch Neubaublöcke prägen das Bild des beschaulichen Stadtteils.

About a quarter of an hour away from the *Demminer Straße* a crane sculpture in front of the café "Elster" greets visitors as the landmark of the popular residential area *Vogelviertel*. With few exceptions, the streets bear the names of birds. Terraced houses, often brick, but also newly built developments characterise the picture of the tranquil neighbourhood.

Rekonstruierte Mehrfamilienhäuser und viele Backsteinhäuser sind charakteristisch für den Stadtteil. Die Bewohner lieben die ruhige und überschaubare Atmosphäre. Die modernisierten Wohnungen im Quartier Fasanenstraße mit schönen Innenhöfen liegen beispielsweise dicht an der Innenstadt und nicht weit entfernt vom Reitbahnsee.

Reconstructed multifamily residences and many brick houses are characteristic of the quarter. The residents love the calm and easy atmosphere. The modernised dwellings at the quarter *Fasanenstraße* with beautiful courtyards are close to the inner city and not far from Lake *Reitbahnsee*.

Auf der Sonnenterrasse am idyllischen Seeufer können sich Junge und Ältere täglich bei Kuchen, Kaffee oder Tee bräunen, entspannen und erholen. Bei Wakeboard-Training oder -Wettkämpfen haben Sportinteressierte eine gute Sicht auf das Geschehen an der Wasserskiseilbahn. Wer Lust und Mut hat, kann es selbst probieren.

On the sun terrace at the idyllic lakefront young and old can sunbathe, relax and recuperate while they have cake, coffee or tea. Sports fans have a good view of what's going on at the water ski ropeway while the wakeboard training and competitions are underway. Anyone with desire and determination can try it themselves.

Eine Runde am Lift misst 845 Meter. An der Fünf-Mast Anlage können zehn Läufer gleichzeitig fahren. Mit einer Geschwindigkeit zwischen 30 km/h und 58 km/h. Die Fachleute empfehlen übrigens, lerne zuerst das Wasserskilaufen, dann ist der Weg auf das Wakeboard deutlich einfacher. Ein Brett, ein Seil und Wasser, ein irres Gefühl.

One circuit with the lift covers 845 metres. The five-mast facility allows ten riders to water ski together with a speed of between 30 km/h and 58 km/h. The specialists recommend learning to water ski first, as this makes the transition onto the wakeboard much easier. A board, a rope and water – a crazy feeling.

Gärten ziehen schon seit Mitte des 18. Jahrhunderts einen grünen Gürtel um die Stadt. Der 1988 gegründete Kleingartenverein Süd-Osthang Datzeberg I hat fünfzig Parzellen mit 32.100 Quadratmetern. Dieser Verein ist einer von 89 in Neubrandenburg. Der erste wurde 1880 in Broda gegründet.

Gardens have drawn a green belt around the town since the middle of the 18th century. The allotment club *Süd-Osthang Datzeberg I*, founded in 1988, has fifty parcels of land with 32,100 square meters. This club is one of 89 in Neubrandenburg. The first one was founded in 1880 in *Broda*.

In Neubrandenburg-Trollenhagen starten und landen militärische wie auch zivile Flugzeuge. Terminal, Tower und Vorfeld hat die Neubrandenburger Flughafengesellschaft in der ersten Hälfte der 1990er Jahre faktisch auf grüner Wiese neu gebaut. Zahlreiche Unternehmer wie Marco Grauel starten gern unweit vom Neubrandenburger Stadtrand.

In *Neubrandenburg-Trollenhagen,* military as well as civil planes take off and land. Neubrandenburg Airport built the terminal, tower and apron in the first half of the 1990s, practically on green fields. Numerous entrepreneurs such as Marco Grauel like to fly from here, close to the Neubrandenburg periphery.

Aus der Luft zeigen Überreste einer gesprengten künstlichen Insel im Tollensesee, was Anliegen der Torpedoforschung und -versuche zwischen 1942 und 1945 war. Hauptaufgabe der Forschungsaußenstelle der Kriegsmarine war das Testen, Einstellen und Einschießen der Torpedos sowie Versuche in der Grundlagenforschung.

From the air the remains of a blown-up artificial island in Lake *Tollense* show the ambitions of the torpedo research and testing between 1942 and 1945. The main task of the navy's research outpost was the testing, adjustment and accuracy of the torpedoes, along with fundamental research.

1905 errichteten die Neubrandenburger auf Behmshöhe im Nemerower Holz einen Aussichtsturm. Der 34 Meter hohe Turm mit seinen 111 Stufen wirkt aus der Vogelperspektive als ein lohnenswertes Ausflugsziel und lässt vom Ostufer einen herrlichen Ausblick auf den Tollensesee und die umliegende Landschaft ahnen.

In 1905 Neubrandenburg erected a look-out tower on *Behmshöhe* in the *Nemerower Holz*. This bird's eye view of the 34m high tower with its 111 steps suggests it will be a worthwhile visit and one can well imagine the magnificent view of Lake *Tollense* and the surrounding landscape from the east bank.